The Live Your Dream Workbook

The LIVE YOUR DREAM *Workbook*

Discover and Live the Life of Your Dreams

BY JOYCE CHAPMAN, M.A.

Newcastle Publishing
North Hollywood, California

The author and publisher of this book do not dispense medical or psychiatric advice, nor prescribe the use of any technique as a form of treatment for medical or psychiatric problems without the advice of a physician or therapist, either directly or indirectly. The intent of this book is to offer information of a general nature to help the reader in his or her quest for emotional well-being. In the event the reader uses the information contained herein for personal therapy, the author and publisher assume no responsibility for this action.

Edited by Gina Gross Misiroglu
Cover and interior design © 1994 Michele Lanci-Altomare

ISBN: 0-87877-195-6
A Newcastle Book
First printing 1994
10 9 8 7 6 5 4 3 2 1
Printed in the United States of America.

This book is dedicated to all those visionaries
who are dreaming big dreams
and working to make them reality.

Contents

Acknowledgments

I want to thank all those whose wonderful books and ideas have helped me to grow, and to invite all those who grow from reading this book to share their experiences with me in writing and help to advance this work. Thank you also to all the "Live Your Dream" workshop participants who with open hearts shared their own growth to enrich this book, and a note of appreciation to Gina Misiroglu and Eva Ditler for their marvelous editing skills. Thanks especially to my family for their unfailing encouragement and for helping make it possible for me to live my dream of creating this book. Finally, my special appreciation goes to Diane Chalfant, who aided me in the production of the original *Live Your Dream* text.

Introduction

The overwhelming response I received from readers who were inspired by my *Live Your Dream* book to recognize and achieve their dreams made me realize that the time was ripe to release *The Live Your Dream Workbook*—a companion book designed to be used in conjunction with the basic text but that can also be used alone.

The exercises in this workbook provide you with the mental preparedness, motivation, theoretical understanding, self-knowledge, and technical ability to discover your own unique life dreams and bring them into full realization. They are arranged in sequence so that as you "work" the book you eliminate your own inner blocks, begin to build your desired life script, and learn the skills necessary to achieve your life purpose.

This workbook gives you solid, proven techniques to mold your life plan so that you can live true to your ultimate potential. The exercises can be used as a personal tool for self-understanding and provide a way for you to take the driver's seat in life.

It is highly recommended that the original *Live Your Dream* book be used along with the workbook to reinforce and assist you along your journey toward self-discovery. This original book is filled with real life stories, comments from students in the Live Your Dream workshop series, sample diagrams and lists, and in-depth explanations to aid you as you work through the exercises. You will find that by using the book as a supplement, you will further enrich the experience of discovering your inner self, evoking change, and becoming whole.

But even if you decide to use this workbook without the basic text, you will discover that by simply giving honest answers to the workbook questions you will be able to remove obstacles, establish new patterns, and successfully create the life that you choose.

So, whether you decide to use the workbook alone as a simple compilation of exercises arranged in a step-by-step approach or side by side with the *Live Your Dream* book, with effort, commitment, and discipline, the Live Your Dream workshop techniques will empower you to live the life of your dreams.

CHAPTER 1

·····················

Defining the Dream

If someone walked up to you and told you, "You can have your life only if you take a step toward living your dream *today*," how would you respond? Well, life *is* saying just that—each and every moment—to you. If you're not busy living to your fullest potential, parts of you are busy fading away.

But discovering and identifying our dreams is often difficult. We are often trained to live according to someone else's idea of what we should be and the inner knowing we once possessed lies buried beneath years and years of suppressing our own wishes and desires. Sometimes we know what our dream is but, because of our fears, we don't pursue it. And, sometimes, we hang onto dead dreams of yesterday that are not valid today.

The journaling questions in this chapter are designed to trigger associations and guide you to your inner knowing of exactly what your dream is. The answers you provide will let your dream surface, take shape, and attain clarity. As you answer these questions, be brutally honest with yourself. You may have to let go of things you've been clinging to or are uncomfortable with to make room for your new, expanded experience. In the process, you will find where your passion lies. You will discover the source of your enthusiasm. As you do the exercises and begin to express aspects of yourself more fully, you will experience a growing sense of inner peace and fulfillment, and a tremendous aliveness and connectedness with life. You will become the *actualized dreamer*.

As you answer these questions and contemplate what your dream means to you, your dream may peak shyly through a crack in your awareness or it may present itself boldly and dramatically. Your challenge as you work your way through this chapter will be to pay attention to the messages you receive from your inner guidance. Remember that you are right where you are supposed to be, and that as you focus on what your dream means to you, the parts of the picture will begin to come into focus, as well. Now, focus on your dream. Enjoy watching it emerge and evolve.

How will I express who I am in this lifetime?

_____

_____

_____

What is the greatest achievement I can imagine myself accomplishing?

_____

_____

What is the greatest contribution I could possibly make?

_____

_____

What is the mark I would make on the world if I were in charge of my life—if there were no reasons or excuses why I couldn't?

_____

_____

What is the greatest me I can imagine being?

_____

_____

What are the implications of living my dream?

_____

_____

_____

_____

_____

Here is a cluster diagram showing chain reactions of the effects that living my dream may have on my life.

"If you don't have a dream, your life will be about your problems." What is my life about today?

_____

_____

_____

What are some of the problems draining my life away?

1. _____

2. _____

3. _____

4. _____

5. _____

6. _____

7. _____

8. _____

What things do I do differently because I am living my dream?

1._____
2._____
3._____
4._____
5._____
6._____
7._____
8._____

Which of my problems of today might become opportunities for learning tomorrow?

1._____
2._____
3._____
4._____
5._____
6._____
7._____
8._____

What messages from within do I want to begin to honor?

1._____
2._____
3._____
4._____
5._____
6._____
7._____
8._____

What parts of my status quo am I most worried about upsetting?

1. _____

2. _____

3. _____

4. _____

5. _____

6. _____

7. _____

8. _____

Where does my passion lie?

_____

_____

_____

_____

_____

_____

_____

_____

What aspects of myself long to be expressed more fully?

1. _____

2. _____

3. _____

4. _____

5. _____

6. _____

7. _____

8. _____

What times have I felt the most alive and connected with life?

1._____
2._____
3._____
4._____
5._____
6._____
7._____
8._____

In what ways am I living according to someone else's idea of what I should be or do or according to someone else's truth?

1._____
2._____
3._____
4._____
5._____
6._____
7._____
8._____

How would my life look if I forgot about being modest and made my own greatest wishes and desires known?

_____
_____

Have I had trouble identifying what my dream is, or have I stalled somewhere along the way to making my dream a reality?

_____

Am I holding onto any dead dreams?

_____

_____

What blocks do I have to doing what I really want to do?

1._____

2._____

3._____

4._____

5._____

6._____

7._____

8._____

What would it take to move beyond each one?

1._____

2._____

3._____

4._____

5._____

6._____

7._____

8._____

What dream job would I like to see become my real job?

_____

_____

_____

What are some potential abilities or interests that I am not expressing?

1. _____
2. _____
3. _____
4. _____
5. _____
6. _____
7. _____
8. _____

How can I express them?

1. _____
2. _____
3. _____
4. _____
5. _____
6. _____
7. _____
8. _____

What are the attributes of the person I desire to be?

1. _____
2. _____
3. _____
4. _____
5. _____
6. _____
7. _____
8. _____

What makes me truly happy?

_____

_____

_____

_____

What do I want?

_____

_____

_____

_____

_____

What do I need?

_____

_____

_____

_____

_____

_____

What actions have I taken today that demonstrate I'm defining my dream?

1._____

2._____

3._____

4._____

5._____

6. _____

7. _____

8. _____

Here's an unedited, uncensored, outrageous description of my dream:

_____

_____

_____

_____

_____

_____

_____

_____

Here's a picture of my dream:

My ideal place to be in nature is:

_____

_____

_____

_____

Here's a sketch of my ideal place to be in nature:

Here's a description of how it feels to be in this place, and what I love about it:

_____

_____

_____

_____

The one quality of this scene that I want to take with me wherever I go is:

_____

_____

_____

_____

As I look at my dream home from the outside, I see:

_____

_____

_____

Inside my dream home, I see and feel:

_____

_____

_____

What objects energize the dreamer in me?

1._____

2._____

3._____

4._____

5._____

6._____

7._____

8._____

As I picture myself expressing my unique talents and doing what I love the most, I see:

_____

_____

The unique contribution I want to make to the world is:

_____

_____

_____

_____

Here's what I absolutely know right now that makes me sure my dream is a real possibility for me to realize:

_____

_____

_____

Here's a vision of my ideal place of work, the surroundings, and people I see:

_____

_____

_____

Here's a list of the rich and plentiful rewards my ideal work brings me:

1. _____
2. _____
3. _____
4. _____
5. _____
6. _____
7. _____
8. _____

Here's a picture of my dream paycheck and the way I plan to apportion it.

As I plan my ultimate business card, here are some words, phrases, colors, and designs I may want to incorporate:

_____

_____

_____

_____

_____

Here's a picture of my ultimate business card:

The plaque that hangs on the wall where I work and tells what I'm all about says:

_____

_____

_____

_____

The feeling states I most treasure and want to fill my days with as I am living my dream are:

1._____

2._____

3._____

4._____

5._____

6._____

7._____

8._____

Which three of these feelings are the most important to me?

1._____

2._____

3._____

My dream statement, in capital letters, is:

_____

_____

_____

_____

My ideal relationship, the one I always longed for, I now have. It's the relationship I have with myself. Here are some of the ways I express my love for myself, and some of the loving thoughts I have about myself:

1._____

2._____

3._____

4._____

5._____

6._____

7._____

8._____

Here's a list of my best qualities—what I appreciate and like most about myself:

1._____
2._____
3._____
4._____
5._____
6._____
7._____
8._____

Someone who knows me well and admires who I am will introduce me in the following way:

_____
_____

Someone who deeply loves me will show that love in the following ways:

1._____
2._____
3._____
4._____
5._____
6._____
7._____
8._____

Here's a description of my best self—the dreamer, the star the world's been waiting for:

_____
_____
_____
_____

Here's one action I will take today, based on knowing the greatest truth about myself and choosing to create my dream:

_____

_____

A description of the ways my dream partner and I interact, empower, and support each other in living our dreams will include:

_____

_____

_____

What do I want to accomplish in this lifetime?

_____

_____

_____

What do I want to be remembered for?

_____

_____

_____

If I could do anything in the world I wanted, what would that be?

_____

_____

_____

What did I dream of being when I was young?

_____

_____

What trophy or award would I like to win? Why?

_____

_____

_____

Whom do I admire? Why?

_____

_____

_____

I will practice the art of *noticing* in my life. For the next three days I will notice the answers to these questions:

What was my first thought upon waking up today?

Day 1. _____

_____

Day 2. _____

_____

Day 3. _____

_____

Am I excited about this day, dreading this day, or is it "just another day"?

Day 1. _____

_____

Day 2. _____

_____

Day 3. _____

_____

What was the most important part of my day today?

Day 1. _____

_____

Day 2. _____

_____

Day 3. _____

_____

What was the most enjoyable part of my day today?

Day 1. _____

_____

Day 2. _____

_____

Day 3. _____

_____

What was it that I willingly set aside to do today?

Day 1. _____

_____

Day 2. _____

_____

Day 3. _____

_____

Has my day been organized in such a way that I will feel satisfied at its end?

Day 1. _____

_____

Day 2. _____

_____

Day 3. _____

_____

What kinds of people did I spend my day with today?

Day 1. _____

_____

Day 2. _____

_____

Day 3. _____

_____

How did these people make me feel—alive, bored, or drained?

Day 1. _____

_____

Day 2. _____

_____

Day 3. _____

_____

Who did I try to impress today?

Day 1. _____

_____

Day 2. _____

_____

Day 3. _____

_____

How much time did I give to spirituality during the day?

Day 1. _____

_____

Day 2. _____

_____

Day 3. _____

_____

Did I live from a higher power today?

Day 1. _____

_____

Day 2. _____

_____

Day 3. _____

_____

Did I put more energy into doubting, worrying, or trusting today?

Day 1. _____

_____

Day 2. _____

_____

Day 3. _____

_____

How does my body feel today—tense, worn out, energetic?

Day 1. _____

_____

Day 2. _____

_____

Day 3. _____

_____

In what moments did I feel fully alive today?

Day 1. _____

_____

Day 2. _____

_____

Day 3. _____

_____

Which activities moved me today to give nothing less than my best?

Day 1. _____

_____

Day 2. _____

_____

Day 3. _____

_____

What did I keep putting off today?

Day 1. _____

_____

Day 2. _____

_____

Day 3. _____

_____

What created real enthusiasm for me today?

Day 1. _____

_____

Day 2. _____

_____

Day 3. _____

_____

What did I appreciate today?

Day 1. _____

_____

Day 2. _____

_____

Day 3. _____

_____

What did I remember today?

Day 1. _____

_____

Day 2. _____

_____

Day 3. _____

_____

What did I forget today?

Day 1. _____

_____

Day 2. _____

_____

Day 3. _____

_____

Who did I put first today?

Day 1. _____

_____

Day 2. _____

_____

Day 3. _____

_____

Who did I put last today?

Day 1. _____

_____

Day 2. _____

_____

Day 3. _____

_____

What did I pay attention to today?

Day 1. _____

_____

Day 2. _____

_____

Day 3. _____

_____

When did I give my power away today?

Day 1. _____

_____

Day 2. _____

_____

Day 3. _____

_____

I will also take note and ponder the answers to these questions.

Am I a positive or negative thinker?

_____

_____

Is money a problem or a joy for me?

_____

Who am I attracted to? Why?

_____

_____

_____

_____

Do my surroundings support me in being my best?

_____

How do I feel when someone asks me what work I do?

_____

_____

_____

_____

What do I work for—money, security, satisfaction?

_____

As I practiced this art of noticing, what insights dawned on me?

1. _____
2. _____
3. _____
4. _____
5. _____
6. _____
7. _____
8. _____

In imagining that I am looking back on my life, nearing its end, I wish I would have:

1. _____
2. _____

3. _____

4. _____

5. _____

6. _____

7. _____

8. _____

What changes do I need to make in my life now, before it is too late?

1. _____

2. _____

3. _____

4. _____

5. _____

6. _____

7. _____

8. _____

I've suddenly found out that I only have a brief time left to live. What will I do with the time I have left?

_____

_____

_____

_____

How is this different from the way I've lived in the last month?

_____

_____

_____

_____

Will my priorities change?

_____

What would become more or less important to me?

_____

_____

_____

_____

What would I want to experience more of, or experience for the first time?

_____

_____

_____

_____

Go back to your definition of your biggest dream. Now that you've completed the exercises for chapter 1 and examined your dream in a more definite way, is there anything you can add to clarify your dream? Take a moment to do that now.

Chapter 1 Dreamwork Checklist

✓ What have I learned from noticing?
✓ How can I be more gentle with myself?
✓ Am I living parts of my dream already?
✓ How do I feel about my life in relation to my dream now?
✓ What concrete steps toward realizing and living my dream have I already taken?
✓ What have I learned from my writing so far?
✓ How do I feel about living my dream so far?
✓ I will say my dream over to myself until it stays on the tip of my tongue.
✓ In this way my dream will soon seem like second nature to me.

CHAPTER 2

....

Clear Away Obstructions to Be Clear About Your Dream

Your new dream requires adjustments in your patterns of living; in other words, in order to make room for a new dream in your life, the first step is to identify whatever interferes with your being able to live your life the way you really want to. You probably have some bad habits, like worry or self-condemnation, that get in the way. On top of that, your spouse, your kids, the bills, the housework, a broken-down car might make your dream seem unachievable. You may even have some beliefs that stop you. For example, your dream is to be a wealthy philanthropist, but you've never met a millionaire who wasn't a power-obsessed tyrant. With a belief like that lurking in your mind, how could you become successful yourself?

In order to make room for your dream in your life, identify whatever interferes with your being able to live the way you really want to. We all have dream inhibitors—bad habits, beliefs that stop us, relationships, distractions. Realize that you are in charge of what stops your dream, and develop alternatives that will empower and support your dream.

The journaling questions in this chapter give you a closer look at whatever is blocking your path toward achieving your dream, help you determine what can be done to overcome the obstacles to living your dream, and aid you in visualizing your dream. Specifically, you'll look at life circumstances that stand in your way of living your dream, and begin to establish a new point of view, a new way of looking at your life situation so that your dream can become a reality.

The questions in this chapter are sequential, each providing a necessary step in putting together the different segments of your particular challenge. Enjoy each step—even those that frustrate you, or make you angry. Anger and frustration are but the opposites of clarity and joy, and those are the states toward which you are heading as you find your dream and begin working on it.

What interferes with my being able to live the way I really want to?

_____

_____

_____

_____

_____

_____

_____

_____

Eight habits that I allow to stand in the way of living my dream:

1. _____
2. _____
3. _____
4. _____
5. _____
6. _____
7. _____
8. _____

New habits that I can use to replace the old dream-defeating ones:

1. _____
2. _____
3. _____
4. _____
5. _____
6. _____

7._____

8._____

Beliefs that I allow to stand in the way of living my dream:

1._____

2._____

3._____

4._____

5._____

6._____

7._____

8._____

Alternatives to each belief I listed that will empower my dream:

1._____

2._____

3._____

4._____

5._____

6._____

7._____

8._____

People I allow to stand in the way of living my dream:

1._____

2._____

3._____

4._____

5. _____

6. _____

7. _____

8. _____

The changes I can make in relation to the people I listed above:

1. _____

2. _____

3. _____

4. _____

5. _____

6. _____

7. _____

8. _____

Things I allow to stand in the way of living my dream:

1. _____

2. _____

3. _____

4. _____

5. _____

6. _____

7. _____

8. _____

Solutions to each item on my distractions list:

1. _____

2. _____

3. _____

4. _____

5. _____

6. _____

7. _____

8. _____

In reading over my answers what common threads or themes do I notice?

_____

_____

_____

_____

_____

_____

What does this suggest to me?

_____

_____

_____

_____

_____

_____

What new decisions will I make?

_____

_____

_____

_____

_____

Fill out the Time Accountant sheet below to determine a list of your activities during each of the seven days of one week.

NUMBER OF HOURS PER DAY								
ACTIVITY	Mon	Tues	Wed	Thurs	Fri	Sat	Sun	Total
Sleep								
Toilette								
Cooking								
Eating								
Exercising								
Travel								
Work								
Telephone/Work								
Telephone/Social								
Interacting/Social								
Leisure								
Entertainment								
Journaling								
Reading								
Television								
Dreamwork								
Other								

What do I observe about the way I spend my time?

_____

_____

_____

_____

_____

_____

_____

What changes can I make to manage my time more optimally?

1._____

2._____

3._____

4._____

5._____

6._____

7._____

8._____

The activities I want to accomplish each day include:

1._____

2._____

3._____

4._____

5._____

6._____

7._____

8._____

Complete the chart below with your dream statement written across the top of the page in large letters and include activity time segments for your ideal day.

TIME SEGMENTS FOR AN IDEAL DAY	
(Your Dream Statement)	
ACTIVITY	**WHEN?**

Over the next four weeks, fill out the following four weekly charts with a key activities list to fit your individual lifestyle. Use a set of colored pencils according to the sample key below to color in each block of time.

SAMPLE KEY		
COLOR	=	**ACTIVITY**
Dark Blue	=	sleep
Yellow	=	morning preparations
Green	=	reading
Gold	=	living my dream and taking steps toward it
Rose	=	journaling
Gray	=	time at office
Pink	=	time on phone at home
Black	=	doing nothing—wasted time
Light Blue	=	watching television
Orange	=	eating
Red	=	playing
Yellow–Green	=	driving, errands
Purple	=	housework
Brown	=	cooking
Fuschia	=	grocery shopping
Aqua	=	visiting
Lavender	=	leisure
White	=	spiritual

SCHEDULING MY DREAM (WEEK ONE)							
HOUR OF DAY	Mon	Tues	Wed	Thurs	Fri	Sat	Sun
5:00–6:00 A.M.							
6:00–7:00							
7:00–8:00							
8:00–9:00							
9:00–10:00							
10:00–11:00							
11:00–12:00							
12:00–1:00 P.M.							
1:00–2:00							
2:00–3:00							
3:00–4:00							
4:00–5:00							
5:00–6:00							
6:00–7:00							
7:00–8:00							
8:00–9:00							
9:00–10:00							
10:00–11:00							
11:00–12:00							
12:00–1:00 A.M.							
1:00–2:00							
2:00–3:00							
3:00–4:00							
4:00–5:00							

What do I observe about my use of time?

_____

_____

_____

SCHEDULING MY DREAM *(WEEK TWO)*

HOUR OF DAY	Mon	Tues	Wed	Thurs	Fri	Sat	Sun
5:00–6:00 A.M.							
6:00–7:00							
7:00–8:00							
8:00–9:00							
9:00–10:00							
10:00–11:00							
11:00–12:00							
12:00–1:00 P.M.							
1:00–2:00							
2:00–3:00							
3:00–4:00							
4:00–5:00							
5:00–6:00							
6:00–7:00							
7:00–8:00							
8:00–9:00							
9:00–10:00							
10:00–11:00							
11:00–12:00							
12:00–1:00 A.M.							
1:00–2:00							
2:00–3:00							
3:00–4:00							
4:00–5:00							

What do I observe about my use of time?

_____

_____

_____

SCHEDULING MY DREAM *(WEEK THREE)*

HOUR OF DAY	Mon	Tues	Wed	Thurs	Fri	Sat	Sun
5:00–6:00 A.M.							
6:00–7:00							
7:00–8:00							
8:00–9:00							
9:00–10:00							
10:00–11:00							
11:00–12:00							
12:00–1:00 P.M.							
1:00–2:00							
2:00–3:00							
3:00–4:00							
4:00–5:00							
5:00–6:00							
6:00–7:00							
7:00–8:00							
8:00–9:00							
9:00–10:00							
10:00–11:00							
11:00–12:00							
12:00–1:00 A.M.							
1:00–2:00							
2:00–3:00							
3:00–4:00							
4:00–5:00							

What do I observe about my use of time?

_____

_____

_____

SCHEDULING MY DREAM *(WEEK FOUR)*

HOUR OF DAY	Mon	Tues	Wed	Thurs	Fri	Sat	Sun
5:00–6:00 A.M.							
6:00–7:00							
7:00–8:00							
8:00–9:00							
9:00–10:00							
10:00–11:00							
11:00–12:00							
12:00–1:00 P.M.							
1:00–2:00							
2:00–3:00							
3:00–4:00							
4:00–5:00							
5:00–6:00							
6:00–7:00							
7:00–8:00							
8:00–9:00							
9:00–10:00							
10:00–11:00							
11:00–12:00							
12:00–1:00 A.M.							
1:00–2:00							
2:00–3:00							
3:00–4:00							
4:00–5:00							

What do I observe about my use of time?

_____

_____

_____

What recommendations do I have for modifying my future use of time?

1. _____
2. _____
3. _____
4. _____
5. _____
6. _____
7. _____
8. _____

What are the things I love and want to bring into reality?

1. _____
2. _____
3. _____
4. _____
5. _____
6. _____
7. _____
8. _____

How do I feel about my use of time?

_____

Is most of my time spent doing what is most important to me?

_____

Am I beginning my day by writing a statement about what I intend to accomplish?

_____

Am I ending my day by following up on it, noting which of my intentions were actually accomplished, and congratulating myself on them?

_____

Does my time chart match my dream?

_____

Is my allocation of my time consistent with my commitment to living my dream?

_____

These are the changes I intend to make:

1._____
2._____
3._____
4._____
5._____
6._____
7._____
8._____

If I could make a collage—a dream board or symbolic visual representation of my dream—using either paste-up magazine cut-out pictures and words or my own drawings and designs, I would like to include:

1._____
2._____
3._____
4._____
5._____
6._____

7. _____

8. _____

Using my above ideas, I will create my own dream board using pictures and words cut out of a magazine (or my own drawings and designs). I will arrange these on a piece of poster board to create an attractive picture of the me I want to be. I will include pictures or photographs of the aspects of my life—my ideal body, family, friends, relationship, home, car, work, accomplishments, finances, leisure activities, vacations—anything and everything that's important to me.

What have I realized from my dream board?

_____

_____

_____

_____

_____

_____

_____

Since I completed and displayed my dream board, I have noticed these conditions around me beginning to move into place to make my dream a reality:

1. _____

2. _____

3. _____

4. _____

5. _____

6. _____

7. _____

8. _____

During conversations with myself in the mirror (about bringing my dream into reality) I will say the following:

1. _____

2. _____

3. _____

4. _____

5. _____

6. _____

7. _____

8. _____

I will call my dream partner every day and read my dream statement as well as a summary of my day's accomplishments.

MY DAY'S ACCOMPLISHMENTS
Name: _____
Dream Partner's Phone Number: _____
My dream statement is:
_____
Day 1: Today I
Day 2: Today I
Day 3: Today I
Day 4: Today I
Day 5: Today I
Day 6: Today I
Day 7: Today I

Now that you've completed chapter 2, you have made an important start. Plan your schedule and stay with it! Acknowledge yourself for your successes. You're doing great!

Chapter 2 Dreamwork Checklist

✓ Visualize your dream each morning. Write down what you have learned by visualizing.
✓ Write down how you go about visualizing.
✓ Write down the difficulties and resistances you encounter.
✓ Schedule and review your goals (dream steps) and progress each day.
✓ Complete all the writing exercises in chapter 2 and chart how you spend your time.
✓ Write a summary of what you learned by charting your time.
✓ Make a dream board and display it prominently.
✓ Hold conversations with your mirror every morning.
✓ Read helpful books.
✓ Call your partner each day and ask:
    What did you do today to live your dream?
    What did you notice and learn from noticing?
    What actions have you taken today about your dream?
✓ Repeat and register for your partner what you heard.
✓ Use phrases like, "I heard..." "I'm not sure..." "Did you say...?" Confront your partner lovingly when necessary.
✓ Write in your journal about insights you receive.

CHAPTER 3

....

A Winning Attitude

Have you ever found yourself in situations where you look around and wonder, How did I ever get here? The simple truth is that we participate, either knowingly or unknowingly, in the process of getting where we are. The more we observe that and pay attention, the more aware we become. It is easier to pretend that we are powerless over the direction our lives are taking—that we are helpless victims—than to accept the truth that we are in control of our own experience. Yet, it is assuming accountability that gives us power over our lives.

The journaling questions in this chapter help you to observe how experiences in your life are caused, directly or indirectly, by various actions you took over the years and by beliefs you may have about yourself. As you answer honestly, you may discover that the powerlessness you sometimes feel now began back when you were four and were sent to live for a time with Aunt Mildred. Or that your unwillingness to joyfully embrace any new job opportunity is based upon not being chosen to play on your favorite sports team. Or that your inability to form fulfilling relationships with the opposite sex was established back in eighth grade when your affections were spurned by a seventh grader.

As silly as it may seem, often your actions and inactions indirectly contributed to the outcome of your present circumstances. The questions (and their answers) are designed to give you practice in acting from a position of responsibility so that you can become the successful manager of your life. The chapter is also a continuation of identifying whatever needs to be completed to free you to live your dream.

As you complete this chapter, if you begin to feel overwhelmed at any point, consult your doctor or a professional therapist. It's possible that reviewing past events will bring up unwanted feelings, and these will need to be addressed with a professional in order to become manageable. The good news is that once you're able to work with "leftover" feelings and beliefs, you'll soon be on your way to taking more control of your life.

What are some of the things that happened to me in the past, that made me feel like a victim?

1. _____
2. _____
3. _____
4. _____
5. _____
6. _____
7. _____
8. _____

How did I react to these situations, what did I think during these situations, and how did I feel in these situations to make me the "helpless victim"?

1. _____
2. _____
3. _____
4. _____
5. _____
6. _____
7. _____
8. _____

How did these reactions, thoughts, and feelings contribute to the outcome of the situation?

1. _____
2. _____
3. _____
4. _____
5. _____
6. _____

7._____

8._____

How could I have reacted, thought, and felt differently so that I would not have been the "helpless victim" in the outcome of the situation?

1._____

2._____

3._____

4._____

5._____

6._____

7._____

8._____

What happened to me today that made me feel like a victim? How did my reactions, feelings, and thoughts contribute to the outcome of the situation? How could I have reacted, felt, or thought differently so that I would not have been the "helpless victim" in this situation?

Day 1. _____

_____

_____

_____

Day 2. _____

_____

_____

_____

Day 3. _____

_____

_____

_____

_____

Day 4. _____

_____

_____

_____

_____

Day 5. _____

_____

_____

_____

_____

Day 6. _____

_____

_____

_____

Day 7. _____

_____

_____

_____

_____

What am I wearing when I imagine myself as a very small child, full of love, joy, playfulness, spontaneity, energy, laughter, and fun?

_____

_____

_____

Where am I playing?

_____

_____

What are the toys I treasure?

_____

_____

_____

What do the caregivers scold me for doing too wildly?

_____

_____

_____

What is my favorite script/story to play?

_____

_____

_____

Who is my audience?

_____

_____

_____

What response does my performance elicit from them?

_____

_____

_____

As a child, what do I love pretending to be?

_____

_____

_____

How do I feel in this imaginary play?

_____

_____

_____

What costumes do I put on?

_____

_____

_____

What part do I play with other kids?

_____

_____

_____

What is my most pleasurable role?

_____

_____

What is it about the experience that I relish so much?

_____

_____

_____

I felt powerful when:

_____

_____

_____

_____

I felt loving when:

_____

_____

_____

_____

I felt playful when:

_____

_____

_____

_____

I felt fully self-expressive when:

_____

_____

_____

_____

I felt productive when:

_____

_____

_____

I felt fully nourished when:

_____

_____

_____

_____

I felt passionately alive when:

_____

_____

_____

_____

I felt responsible and important when:

_____

_____

_____

_____

I felt joyful when:

_____

_____

_____

_____

What did each of these experiences mean to me?

_____

_____

_____

_____

_____

_____

What conclusions did I draw from it at the time?

_____

_____

_____

_____

After pondering these questions, what insights can I draw from my answers?

_____

_____

_____

_____

When was the first time that I decided that it was not okay to be who I am?

_____

_____

_____

_____

What would happen if I dared to be the real me today?

_____

_____

_____

_____

Which experiences and which qualities would I choose to reclaim?

1. _____
2. _____
3. _____
4. _____
5. _____
6. _____
7. _____
8. _____

How would I act if I knew I had nothing to lose? How outrageous would I be?

_____
_____
_____
_____

In working the above questions, I came up with this single sentence that summarizes my insights:

_____
_____
_____
_____

What are some of the things in my life that are incomplete?

1. _____
2. _____
3. _____
4. _____
5. _____

6. _____

7. _____

8. _____

What relationships do I have in which I feel an incompleteness?

1. _____

2. _____

3. _____

4. _____

5. _____

6. _____

7. _____

8. _____

What feels incomplete in this relationship?

1. _____

_____

_____

2. _____

_____

_____

3. _____

_____

_____

4. _____

_____

_____

5. _____

_____

_____

6. _____

_____

_____

7. _____

_____

_____

8. _____

_____

_____

What have I been intending to get done in this relationship?

1. _____

_____

_____

2. _____

_____

_____

3. _____

_____

_____

4. _____

_____

_____

5. _____

_____

_____

6. _____

_____

_____

7. _____

_____

_____

8. _____

_____

_____

What have I been putting off in this relationship?

1. _____

_____

_____

2. _____

_____

_____

3. _____

_____

_____

4. _____

_____

_____

5. _____

_____

_____

6. _____

_____

_____

7. _____

8. _____

_____

_____

What truths have been left uncommunicated in this relationship?

1. _____

_____

_____

2. _____

_____

_____

3. _____

_____

_____

4. _____

_____

_____

5. _____

_____

_____

6. _____

_____

_____

7. _____

_____

_____

8. _____

_____

_____

What messages need to be delivered in this relationship?

1. _____

_____

_____

2. _____

_____

_____

3. _____

_____

_____

4. _____

_____

_____

5. _____

_____

_____

6. _____

_____

_____

7. _____

_____

_____

8. _____

_____

_____

What regrets, resentments, hurts, criticisms, and apologies have been withheld in this relationship?

1. _____

_____

_____

2. _____

_____

_____

3. _____

_____

_____

4. _____

_____

_____

5. _____

_____

_____

6. _____

_____

_____

7. _____

_____

_____

8. _____

_____

_____

What stands between me and this person?

1. _____

_____

2._____

_____

3._____

_____

4._____

_____

5._____

_____

6._____

_____

7._____

_____

8._____

_____

What prevents me from being completely open and honest with this person?

1._____

_____

2._____

_____

3. _____

4. _____

5. _____

6. _____

7. _____

8. _____

What keeps the two of us from meeting each other's eyes unguardedly?

1. _____

2. _____

3. _____

4._____

_____

_____

5._____

_____

_____

6._____

_____

_____

7._____

_____

_____

8._____

_____

_____

What lies, half-truths, and withheld truths need to be cleaned up in this relationship?

1._____

_____

_____

2._____

_____

_____

3._____

_____

_____

4._____

_____

5. _____

_____

_____

6. _____

_____

_____

7. _____

_____

_____

8. _____

_____

_____

What broken promises and agreements need to be acknowledged and resolved, either by keeping them or by making a new agreement?

1. _____

_____

_____

2. _____

_____

_____

3. _____

_____

_____

4. _____

_____

_____

5. _____

_____

_____

6. _____

_____

_____

7. _____

_____

_____

8. _____

_____

_____

What can I do to repair or resolve any damaged relationships?

1. _____

_____

_____

2. _____

_____

_____

3. _____

_____

_____

4. _____

_____

_____

5. _____

_____

_____

6. _____

_____

_____

7._____

_____

_____

8._____

_____

_____

Do I need to forgive someone?

_____

_____

_____

What amends do I want to make, if my actions have hurt or damaged someone else?

_____

_____

_____

_____

Is there a relationship that has died or become injurious and needs to be ended?

_____

_____

_____

What acknowledgments do I want to give to people who have made special contributions to my life?

_____

_____

Here is a list of letters I will write, phone calls I will make, and talks I will have in person:

1. _____
2. _____
3. _____
4. _____
5. _____
6. _____
7. _____
8. _____

As far as my physical body is concerned, what feels incomplete in the areas of: (1) dieting; (2) health; (3) exercise; (4) clothing; and (5) personal appearance?

1. _____

_____

2. _____

_____

3. _____

_____

4. _____

_____

5. _____

_____

What have I been intending to get done in the areas of: (1) dieting; (2) health; (3) exercise; (4) clothing; and (5) personal appearance?

1. _____
2. _____

3._____

4._____

5._____

What have I been putting off in the areas of: (1) dieting; (2) health; (3) exercise; (4) clothing; and (5) personal appearance?

1._____

2._____

3._____

4._____

5._____

What actions do I want to take to make my body a reliable vehicle to support my dream plans?

_____

_____

_____

_____

_____

_____

_____

Is my general appearance appropriate for someone who is living my dream?

_____

_____

_____

_____

_____

_____

What concrete actions will I take?

1. _____
2. _____
3. _____
4. _____
5. _____
6. _____
7. _____
8. _____

When did I last have a physical exam?

_____
_____
_____
_____

Have I been putting off dental work, medical treatment, or an eye exam?

_____

What skin care products or treatments are in order?

_____
_____
_____
_____

How is my hearing?

_____
_____

What is my plan for an exercise routine?

_____

_____

_____

_____

How will I implement it and reward myself when I follow through?

_____

_____

_____

_____

What concrete steps will I take to improve my overall health?

1. _____
2. _____
3. _____
4. _____
5. _____
6. _____
7. _____
8. _____

Do I have any type of addiction (cigarettes, alcohol, drugs, food)? If so, what concrete steps will I take to overcome my addiction?

1. _____
2. _____
3. _____
4. _____
5. _____

6. _____

7. _____

8. _____

What pleases me about my wardrobe?

_____

_____

What negative reactions do I have with regard to my wardrobe?

_____

_____

What concrete steps can I take to create the wardrobe of my dreams?

1. _____

2. _____

3. _____

4. _____

5. _____

6. _____

7. _____

8. _____

In the area of my finances what feels incomplete about my…

Income: _____

_____

Investments: _____

_____

Savings: _____

Checkbook:_____

Insurance:_____

Taxes:_____

Financial planning:_____

Records:_____

Debts:_____

Bills:_____

What have I been intending to get done in the areas of…

Income:_____

Investments:_____

Savings:_____

Checkbook:_____

Insurance:_____

Taxes:_____

Financial planning: _____

Records: _____

Debts: _____

Bills: _____

What have I been putting off in the areas of...

Income: _____

Investments: _____

Savings: _____

Checkbook: _____

Insurance: _____

Taxes: _____

Financial planning: _____

Records: _____

Debts: _____

Bills:_____

_____

Is my current income enough or do I need to find a way to increase it?

_____

If I need to find a way to increase it, what will I do?

_____

_____

_____

_____

_____

Is my checkbook balanced?

_____

Is my money being handled the way it will need to be handled when I am living my dream?

_____

Are my tax records current?

_____

Do I owe taxes?

_____

Do I need some help figuring or managing my taxes?

_____

Are my tax files organized and accessible?

_____

What else needs to be done to organize my financial records and bring them up to date?

_____

_____

_____

_____

Would a money management class serve me well?

_____

When did I last review the coverage and rates on each of my insurance policies?

_____

Have members of my household been informed about these policies and where they are kept?

_____

What actions do I need to take to prepare for later years—retirement, personal investment plans?

_____

_____

As far as my leisure time is concerned, what feels incomplete in the areas of...

Leisure time savings:_____

_____

Leisure time plans: _____

_____

Games/sports: _____

_____

Reading: _____

_____

What have I been intending to get done in the areas of...

Leisure time savings: _____

_____

Leisure time plans: _____

_____

Games/sports: _____

_____

Reading: _____

_____

What have I been putting off in the areas of...

Leisure time savings: _____

_____

Leisure time plans: _____

_____

Games/sports: _____

_____

Reading: _____

_____

Am I making adequate time for leisure activities?

_____

What enjoyable ways of relaxing have I been putting off?

_____

_____

_____

What games or equipment do I want to purchase?

_____

_____

_____

What vacation/leisure plans do I want to arrange?

_____

_____

_____

What changes can I make in my home and schedule to enable me to enjoy my leisure time more?

_____

_____

_____

What kind of recreation do I want more of?

_____

_____

_____

What people and places would I like to visit?

_____

_____

_____

What friends and family members would I enjoy spending more time with?

_____

_____

_____

What kind of fun do I wish I had more of?

_____

_____

_____

What makes me laugh?

_____

_____

_____

What kinds of activities do I put off until vacation or retirement time, when I could be enjoying them now?

_____

_____

_____

As far as my home is concerned, what feels incomplete in these areas...

Yard:_____

_____

Cleaning: _____

_____

Remodeling: _____

_____

Spare bedroom: _____

_____

Garage: _____

_____

Projects: _____

_____

What have I been intending to get done in these areas...

Yard: _____

_____

Cleaning: _____

_____

Remodeling: _____

_____

Spare bedroom: _____

_____

Garage: _____

_____

Projects: _____

_____

What have I been putting off in these areas...

Yard: _____

_____

Cleaning: _____

_____

Remodeling: _____

_____

Spare bedroom: _____

_____

Garage: _____

_____

Projects: _____

_____

What do I no longer use in my home that I can give away?

_____

_____

_____

_____

What repairs are needed?

_____

_____

What appliances need to be fixed or replaced?

_____

_____

What maintenance work should be done?

_____

_____

What remodeling projects are pending or necessary?

_____

_____

What items have I borrowed that need to be returned?

_____

_____

_____

What items have I lent out that need to be retrieved?

_____

_____

_____

Are there magazine subscriptions that I should cancel?

_____

Is there anything that needs to be done to the exterior of my house, yard, or garden?

_____

Do windows, doors, and locks need repair or replacement?

_____

What will it take to restore my car to perfect order?

_____

_____

_____

_____

Do I need a new car?

_____

_____

As far as my work is concerned, what feels incomplete in the areas of…

Relationships:_____

_____

Desk: _____

_____

Equipment: _____

_____

Plans:_____

_____

Projects: _____

_____

What have I been intending to get done in the areas of…

Work relationships:_____

_____

Desk: _____

_____

Work equipment: _____

_____

Work plans: _____

_____

Work projects:_____

_____

What have I been putting off in the areas of...

Work relationships:_____
_____

Desk: _____
_____

Work equipment: _____
_____

Work plans: _____
_____

Work projects:_____
_____

What tasks at work have been left unhandled?
_____
_____

Is my work schedule manageable?
_____

Is my office a mess?
_____

Do certain jobs seem to wait stacked up on my desk forever?
_____

When was the last time I cleaned out my files?
_____

How orderly is my desk?

_____

What changes can I make at work, to create an ideal place where I can live my dream?

_____

_____

_____

Have I been intending to ask for a raise?

_____

Are my travel and expense reimbursement forms up to date?

_____

What about other records I am responsible for keeping?

_____

_____

_____

What meetings need to be scheduled?

_____

_____

_____

What equipment needs repair?

_____

_____

_____

What improvements would I recommend?

_____

_____

_____

_____

What have I been wanting to communicate to my employer, my employees, or my co-workers?

_____

_____

_____

_____

As far as self-improvement is concerned, what feels incomplete in the areas of...

Classes: _____

_____

Reading: _____

_____

Counseling: _____

_____

Travel: _____

_____

Journaling: _____

_____

What have I been intending to get done in the areas of...

Classes: _____

_____

Reading: _____

_____

Counseling: _____

_____

Travel: _____

_____

Journaling: _____

_____

What have I been putting off?

Classes: _____

_____

Reading: _____

_____

Counseling: _____

_____

Travel: _____

_____

Journaling: _____

_____

What are the ways I'd like to improve myself?

1. _____
2. _____
3. _____
4. _____
5. _____
6. _____

7. _____

8. _____

Might I benefit from some personal counseling? Why?

_____

Would I like to use a personal image consultant? Why?

_____

What personal growth seminars do I want to take?

_____

_____

_____

_____

_____

Are there educational classes I would like to take?

_____

_____

_____

_____

_____

What are the books I've been wanting to read?

_____

_____

_____

_____

What are the audio tapes/video tapes I've been wanting to buy?

_____

_____

_____

_____

_____

_____

Is there a church or synagogue I've been meaning to attend?

_____

_____

_____

By cleaning out and handling things, I:

1._____

2._____

3._____

4._____

5._____

6._____

7._____

8._____

What does excellence mean to me?

_____

_____

_____

_____

In what one area of my life have I come closest to experiencing true excellence?

_____

_____

_____

_____

_____

How did this come about?

_____

_____

_____

_____

What other experiences came close?

_____

_____

_____

_____

_____

In which areas do I need to develop excellence to live my dream?

1._____

2._____

3._____

4._____

5._____

6._____

7._____

8._____

What steps will I need to take to achieve excellence in each area?

1. _____

2. _____

3. _____

4. _____

5. _____

6. _____

7. _____

8. _____

What specialized skills will require excellence in the areas I wish to be?

_____

_____

_____

_____

_____

_____

_____

Why?

_____

_____

_____

_____

_____

_____

_____

_____

How?

_____

_____

_____

_____

_____

_____

_____

Eight positive statements about myself that replace old, negative, self-defeating thoughts:

1._____
2._____
3._____
4._____
5._____
6._____
7._____
8._____

Eight affirmations of my own to empower my dream:

1._____
2._____
3._____
4._____
5._____
6._____
7._____
8._____

In completing chapter 3, remember to strive for a winning attitude that will help you rise confidently to meet the challenges and greet the opportunities that you must face along the road to your dream. Take responsibility and be committed to completing things.

Chapter 3 Dreamwork Checklist

✓ Teach the "victim" to take responsibility.
✓ Let the child in you come out to play.
✓ Be committed to completing things.
✓ Celebrate completion!
✓ Build a winning attitude.
✓ Read your affirmations each morning and night.
✓ Call your dream partner. You are a dream doctor: give your partner a prescription for the next week, to help your partner move toward his or her dream.
✓ Each day when you call your partner, reinforce each other for your progress and your completions.
✓ Share your accomplishments and whether you carried through with your scheduled plan.
✓ Keep up the mirror image conversations every morning.
✓ Put your dream board up and look at it often. Add to it as your dreams grow.
✓ Continue visualizing twice daily—see yourself living your dream.
✓ Continue daily scheduling, recording your plan for each day, what you want out of the day, and note your successes in carrying out your plan.

CHAPTER 4

....

Taking Inventory and Taking Charge

In order to cultivate your dream and ensure its hardy growth, you need to continually nourish it and protect it from disturbance or invasion. To do that, you need to understand yourself better, so that you can continually "feed" your dream with yourself. In this next step of living your dream you will have the opportunity to analyze your most basic characteristics, find out what motivates you, learn how to build more motivators in your life, identify which talents come naturally to you, and discover how to put your values, motivators, and talents to work for you.

Through the journaling questions in this chapter you'll take an in-depth personal inventory and, as you work in these areas, find yourself moving closer and closer to knowing for sure who you truly are. You will begin living in harmony with the real inside *you*. And once you are comfortable with the reality of that, you will discover how you can become *more* of what you already are. This is the you that you'll want to express more fully and more joyously, within yourself, to your friends and family, and out in the world. Final questions in this chapter aid you in developing a plan for accomplishing your dream based upon who you really are. In the process, you begin *becoming* your dream.

What did I learn from creating my dream board?

_____

_____

_____

_____

What did I learn from working with my dream partner?

_____

_____

_____

_____

Have you started keeping a journal to record your learning and observations?

_____

_____

_____

_____

What did I learn from my mirror image conversations?

_____

_____

_____

_____

What have I learned from my daily scheduling?

_____

_____

_____

What have I learned about the blockages I create in my life?

_____

_____

_____

_____

What do I find myself doing most often?

_____

_____

_____

_____

How do I spend my time?

_____

_____

_____

_____

What do I talk about?

_____

_____

_____

_____

What do I do when I have a day off?

_____

_____

_____

What offends my sense of justice and provokes indignation and outrage?

_____

_____

_____

_____

Which of my values am I the most proud of?

1._____

2._____

3._____

4._____

5._____

6._____

7._____

8._____

If I set out to select the values that would best help me realize my dream, what would they be?

1._____

2._____

3._____

4._____

5._____

6._____

7._____

8._____

How would I complete the sentence, "Under no condition would I ever _____?"

_____

What is the closest I have come to confronting my ultimate truth?

_____

_____

_____

_____

What is the single most important value I stand for in my life?

_____

_____

_____

_____

In what ways do I demonstrate this?

_____

_____

_____

_____

What value is at the core of my reason for being?

_____

_____

_____

_____

What concrete actions have I taken in the past week that show the importance I give this value?

1._____

2._____

3._____

4._____

5._____

6._____

7._____

8._____

How does this value fit into living my dream?

_____

_____

_____

Here is a list of my most important values:

1._____

2._____

3._____

4._____

5._____

6._____

7._____

8._____

Have my actions in the past week been true to my values?

_____

_____

_____

Here is a list of the actions I have taken in the past week that have been true to my values:

1._____

2._____

3._____

4._____

5._____

6._____

7._____

8._____

Here is a list of actions that I have taken in the past week that have not been true to my values:

1._____

2._____

3._____

4._____

5._____

6._____

7._____

8._____

What do the two questions above teach me about my values?

_____

_____

_____

What work is needed to bring myself into alignment with my values?

_____

_____

_____

_____

Check off the values that apply to you from the list below:

❑ Integrity ❑ Freedom ❑ Wisdom ❑ Inner Peace ❑ Meaningful Work

❑ Humor ❑ Nature ❑ Spirituality ❑ Order ❑ Intelligence

❑ Fitness ❑ Excellence ❑ Learning ❑ Competence ❑ Service to Others

❑ Spontaneity ❑ Creativity ❑ Economy ❑ Simplicity ❑ Self-expression

❑ Comfort ❑ Security ❑ Faith ❑ Trust ❑ Companionship

❑ Balance ❑ Love ❑ Beauty ❑ Power ❑ Relationships

❑ Self-discipline ❑ _____ ❑ _____ ❑ _____

As I go over this list, the five most important values in my life right now are:

1._____

2._____

3._____

4._____

5._____

How did I choose these and why?

1._____

2._____

3._____

4._____

5._____

What top values would I choose if my most important priority were to bring my dream into reality?

1._____

2._____

3._____

4._____

5._____

What do I need to value most highly to make my dream possible?

_____

_____

_____

Why did I pick these values to make my dream possible?

1._____

_____

2._____

_____

3._____

_____

4._____

_____

5._____

_____

What changes do I need to make in my current lifestyle to bring about these values and make my dream possible?

_____

_____

_____

In the last thirty minutes these are the thoughts that ran through my mind:

_____

_____

_____

_____

_____

Of those thoughts, these are the thoughts that support the values I listed:

_____

_____

_____

_____

_____

Of those thoughts, these are the thoughts that do not support the values I listed:

_____

_____

_____

_____

_____

Am I living out of the values my dream represents?

_____

Here is a dialogue between myself and my parents on the subject of values:

_____

_____

_____

_____

_____

_____

_____

_____

_____

_____

What I am going to need to value to live a dream like mine?

_____

_____

_____

How will I demonstrate my values to the world?

_____

_____

_____

_____

_____

_____

_____

_____

_____

What are the steps I need to take to go the full distance for my dream?

1. _____

2. _____

3. _____

4. _____

5. _____

6._____

7._____

8._____

Which of my top five values involve inner-directed motivators?

1._____

2._____

3._____

4._____

5._____

Which of my top five values involve other-directed motivators?

1._____

2._____

3._____

4._____

5._____

What do I think about this?

_____

_____

_____

_____

What choices can I make to increase inner-directed motivation?

1._____

2._____

3._____

4. _____

5. _____

6. _____

7. _____

8. _____

Do I associate inner-directed motivation with selfishness?

_____

_____

_____

Here is a list of what motivates me most:

1. _____

2. _____

3. _____

4. _____

5. _____

6. _____

7. _____

8. _____

What rewards are motivating for me?

1. _____

2. _____

3. _____

4. _____

5. _____

6. _____

7.＿＿＿＿＿＿＿＿＿＿＿＿＿＿＿＿＿＿＿＿＿＿＿＿＿＿＿＿＿＿＿＿＿＿＿

8.＿＿＿＿＿＿＿＿＿＿＿＿＿＿＿＿＿＿＿＿＿＿＿＿＿＿＿＿＿＿＿＿＿＿＿

What feelings do I prize?

1.＿＿＿＿＿＿＿＿＿＿＿＿＿＿＿＿＿＿＿＿＿＿＿＿＿＿＿＿＿＿＿＿＿＿＿

2.＿＿＿＿＿＿＿＿＿＿＿＿＿＿＿＿＿＿＿＿＿＿＿＿＿＿＿＿＿＿＿＿＿＿＿

3.＿＿＿＿＿＿＿＿＿＿＿＿＿＿＿＿＿＿＿＿＿＿＿＿＿＿＿＿＿＿＿＿＿＿＿

4.＿＿＿＿＿＿＿＿＿＿＿＿＿＿＿＿＿＿＿＿＿＿＿＿＿＿＿＿＿＿＿＿＿＿＿

5.＿＿＿＿＿＿＿＿＿＿＿＿＿＿＿＿＿＿＿＿＿＿＿＿＿＿＿＿＿＿＿＿＿＿＿

6.＿＿＿＿＿＿＿＿＿＿＿＿＿＿＿＿＿＿＿＿＿＿＿＿＿＿＿＿＿＿＿＿＿＿＿

7.＿＿＿＿＿＿＿＿＿＿＿＿＿＿＿＿＿＿＿＿＿＿＿＿＿＿＿＿＿＿＿＿＿＿＿

8.＿＿＿＿＿＿＿＿＿＿＿＿＿＿＿＿＿＿＿＿＿＿＿＿＿＿＿＿＿＿＿＿＿＿＿

What sensations would I travel to the ends of the earth for in order to claim as my own?

1.＿＿＿＿＿＿＿＿＿＿＿＿＿＿＿＿＿＿＿＿＿＿＿＿＿＿＿＿＿＿＿＿＿＿＿

2.＿＿＿＿＿＿＿＿＿＿＿＿＿＿＿＿＿＿＿＿＿＿＿＿＿＿＿＿＿＿＿＿＿＿＿

3.＿＿＿＿＿＿＿＿＿＿＿＿＿＿＿＿＿＿＿＿＿＿＿＿＿＿＿＿＿＿＿＿＿＿＿

4.＿＿＿＿＿＿＿＿＿＿＿＿＿＿＿＿＿＿＿＿＿＿＿＿＿＿＿＿＿＿＿＿＿＿＿

5.＿＿＿＿＿＿＿＿＿＿＿＿＿＿＿＿＿＿＿＿＿＿＿＿＿＿＿＿＿＿＿＿＿＿＿

6.＿＿＿＿＿＿＿＿＿＿＿＿＿＿＿＿＿＿＿＿＿＿＿＿＿＿＿＿＿＿＿＿＿＿＿

7.＿＿＿＿＿＿＿＿＿＿＿＿＿＿＿＿＿＿＿＿＿＿＿＿＿＿＿＿＿＿＿＿＿＿＿

8.＿＿＿＿＿＿＿＿＿＿＿＿＿＿＿＿＿＿＿＿＿＿＿＿＿＿＿＿＿＿＿＿＿＿＿

What insights do these answers give me?

1.＿＿＿＿＿＿＿＿＿＿＿＿＿＿＿＿＿＿＿＿＿＿＿＿＿＿＿＿＿＿＿＿＿＿＿

2.＿＿＿＿＿＿＿＿＿＿＿＿＿＿＿＿＿＿＿＿＿＿＿＿＿＿＿＿＿＿＿＿＿＿＿

3.＿＿＿＿＿＿＿＿＿＿＿＿＿＿＿＿＿＿＿＿＿＿＿＿＿＿＿＿＿＿＿＿＿＿＿

4.＿＿＿＿＿＿＿＿＿＿＿＿＿＿＿＿＿＿＿＿＿＿＿＿＿＿＿＿＿＿＿＿＿＿＿

5. _____
6. _____
7. _____
8. _____

What do I want my tombstone to say?

_____
_____

What are my personal positive motivators?

1. _____
2. _____
3. _____
4. _____
5. _____
6. _____
7. _____
8. _____

In what ways can I build more motivators into my life?

1. _____
2. _____
3. _____
4. _____
5. _____
6. _____
7. _____
8. _____

Here is my personal plan for making those rewards that motivate me a part of the realization of my dream:

_____

_____

_____

_____

_____

Have I been living my life out of choices and decisions that I made long ago?

_____

In what way?

_____

_____

_____

What are some new ways of being that are more congruent with myself of today?

1._____

2._____

3._____

4._____

5._____

6._____

7._____

8._____

Which talents come naturally to me?

_____

_____

_____

_____

What do I do well?

_____

_____

_____

_____

From some of the activities that I recently completed, I can acknowledge myself for:

1._____

2._____

3._____

4._____

5._____

6._____

7._____

8._____

Some compliments I can give myself are:

1._____

2._____

3._____

4._____

5._____

6._____

7._____

8._____

What did I like to do most as a young child?

_____

_____

_____

What words did I use to ask questions?

_____

_____

_____

Was I interested in understanding people, nature, intellectual concepts, or mechanical objects?

_____

What was I good at doing at home and at school?

_____

_____

_____

Here is a list of things that I do very well now, broken down into separate components, that I particularly enjoy:

1. _____
2. _____
3. _____
4. _____
5. _____
6. _____
7. _____
8. _____

Here is a list of experiences I've had recently which made me feel vitally alive, with an identification of what it was about the experience that made me feel so good:

1._____

2._____

3._____

4._____

5._____

Here is a list of activities that give me so much energy nothing else matters when I'm doing them:

1._____

2._____

3._____

4._____

5._____

Here is a recollection of two experiences I've had lately when I felt absolute joy, and examples of how I brought these experiences about:

1._____

_____

_____

_____

_____

_____

2._____

_____

_____

_____

_____

_____

When do I feel the happiest?

_____

_____

_____

_____

_____

_____

_____

_____

What are some specific characteristics that I would want to express in the perfect job for me?

_____

_____

_____

_____

_____

_____

_____

_____

How will my natural talents and skills be used in this perfect job?

_____

_____

_____

_____

_____

_____

_____

_____

If two of my best friends were talking to each other about me, eight wonderful things they would say about me would be:

1. _____
2. _____
3. _____
4. _____
5. _____
6. _____
7. _____
8. _____

As far as my physical body is concerned, my ideal self will be…

My entire lifetime: _____
_____

Ten years: _____
_____

Five years: _____
_____

One year: _____
_____

Six months: _____
_____

Three months: _____
_____

I will accomplish this by taking these actions…

My entire lifetime: _____

_____

Ten years: _____

_____

Five years: _____

_____

One year: _____

_____

Six months: _____

_____

Three months:_____

_____

As far as my relationships are concerned, my ideal self will be…

My entire lifetime: _____

_____

Ten years: _____

_____

Five years: _____

_____

One year: _____

_____

Six months: _____

_____

Three months:_____

_____

I will accomplish this by taking these actions…

My entire lifetime: _____

_____

Ten years: _____

_____

Five years: _____

_____

One year: _____

_____

Six months: _____

_____

Three months:_____

_____

As far as my career is concerned, my ideal self will be…

My entire lifetime: _____

_____

Ten years: _____

_____

Five years: _____

_____

One year: _____

_____

Six months: _____

_____

Three months:_____

_____

I will accomplish this by taking these actions…

My entire lifetime: _____

_____

Ten years: _____

_____

Five years: _____

_____

One year: _____

_____

Six months: _____

_____

Three months:_____

_____

As far as my work and home environment is concerned, my ideal self will be…

My entire lifetime: _____

_____

Ten years: _____

_____

Five years: _____

_____

One year: _____

_____

Six months: _____

_____

Three months:_____

_____

I will accomplish this by taking these actions…

My entire lifetime: _____

_____

Ten years: _____

_____

Five years: _____

_____

One year: _____

_____

Six months: _____

_____

Three months:_____

_____

As far as my mental state of being is concerned, my ideal self will be…

My entire lifetime: _____

_____

Ten years: _____

_____

Five years: _____

_____

One year: _____

_____

Six months: _____

_____

Three months:_____

_____

I will accomplish this by taking these actions…

My entire lifetime: _____

_____

Ten years: _____

_____

Five years: _____

_____

One year: _____

_____

Six months: _____

_____

Three months:_____

_____

As far as my spiritual life is concerned, my ideal self will be…

My entire lifetime: _____

_____

Ten years: _____

_____

Five years: _____

_____

One year: _____

_____

Six months: _____

_____

Three months:_____

_____

I will accomplish this by taking these actions...

My entire lifetime: _____

_____

Ten years: _____

_____

Five years: _____

_____

One year: _____

_____

Six months: _____

_____

Three months:_____

_____

As far as my financial well-being is concerned, my ideal self will be...

My entire lifetime: _____

_____

Ten years: _____

_____

Five years: _____

_____

One year: _____

_____

Six months: _____

_____

Three months:_____

_____

I will accomplish this by taking these actions…

My entire lifetime: _____

_____

Ten years: _____

_____

Five years: _____

_____

One year: _____

_____

Six months: _____

_____

Three months:_____

_____

As far as my leisure/recreation time is concerned, my ideal self will be…

My entire lifetime: _____

_____

Ten years: _____

_____

Five years: _____

_____

One year: _____

_____

Six months: _____

_____

Three months:_____

_____

I will accomplish this by taking these actions...

My entire lifetime: _____

_____

Ten years: _____

_____

Five years: _____

_____

One year: _____

_____

Six months: _____

_____

Three months:_____

_____

★ ★

In chapter 4 you stated your dream plan and identified its working stages. This has set in motion the process of realizing your dream. As you continue doing the work necessary to keep to your schedule, look at your dream plan periodically. You may decide to change parts of your dream. You will undoubtedly be astonished at the progress you have made, if you truly commit yourself to each aspect of your dream.

Chapter 4 Dreamwork Checklist

✓ Spend 15 minutes daily visualizing yourself living your dream, and write your thoughts in your journal.
✓ Keep reading your affirmations, morning and night.
✓ Make a list of the steps you've taken so far toward realizing your dream. List completed items, steps accomplished in them, successes and milestones.
✓ Live according to your values. Pay attention to whether you are doing this or not.

✓ Build inner-directed motivators into your everyday life.
✓ Acknowledge yourself often, and deliberately build your self-esteem. Acknowledge others, too.
✓ Think about and list activities that bring you joy and aliveness.
✓ Work with your dream partner to repeatedly drill each other on the question, "What are you best at?" Give quick, spontaneous responses—whatever pops into your mind.
✓ Add one item every day to your list of natural gifts and talents.
✓ Outline the specifications of your ideal job.
✓ Create your dream plan, and begin to work on it.
✓ Create an imaginative visual display showing the steps and stages of your dream plan.
✓ Call your dream partner five times a week and ask how you can assist him or her in living according to his or her values. Share what motivators are influencing you right now, and ask about your partner's dream plan progress.

CHAPTER 5

....

Your Power to Turn Negatives into Positives

Problems or challenges appear in our lives from time to time, yet it is not the problem that can make or break us; it is what we make of it. Do you look at your difficulties with appreciation or regret? Handicaps can turn into victories; challenges can turn into growth experiences. This chapter helps you turn your energy into making your problem situation a winning one. Turning a handicap into a victory is the stuff from which heroes are made— you've seen the movies, read the books, dreamed some of the same dreams—and you can do it, too, from one moment to the next, starting now.

Challenges often do turn into growth experiences. The journaling questions in this chapter give you an opportunity to practice techniques that can enable you to make the most of every situation you're involved in and turn negatives into positives. Sometimes difficulties are a learning tool. The questions in this chapter help you discover the learning within problems, give you techniques to release yourself from being stuck in a problem, and help you find its gift instead. Working this chapter enables you to get clear and focused on what you want. Practice exercises are included to help you enliven your language and choose more empowering words to turn negativity around.

As you work through these exercises, remember that it is time for you to stop suffering and struggling, to relax and peacefully accept your feelings, your challenges, your life situation *exactly as it is* today. Turn your energy into making your problem situation a winning one, with a slight attitude adjustment: mentally release your negativity and make a concerted effort to see the positive side of your situation, a side to which you can bring joy, and laughter, a side that is a step toward resolution.

Do I look at difficulties with appreciation or regret?

_____

Do I want to turn negatives into positives?

_____

What useful purpose does my suffering and resistance to change serve?

_____

_____

_____

Do I need it to grow stronger in some way?

_____

The harder I struggle and suffer do I learn more?

_____

Here is a recollection of a time when conflict taught me something:

_____

_____

_____

_____

_____

Here are three problems I am now facing, written in third-person narrative:
1._____

_____

_____

_____

_____

2._____

_____

_____

_____

_____

3._____

_____

_____

_____

_____

What am I learning from these problems?

1._____

_____

2._____

_____

3._____

_____

What advice might I give to someone else facing these circumstances?

1._____

_____

2._____

_____

3._____

_____

These are three childhood memories that seemed to be negative but which I am now writing as positive experiences from a third person narrative:

1. _____

_____

_____

_____

2. _____

_____

_____

_____

3. _____

_____

_____

_____

If I create the "storm," what purpose is it serving for me now?

_____

_____

_____

What can I learn?

_____

_____

_____

_____

What is to be gained from the difficulty I must face?

_____

_____

_____

_____

What do I need to do, to clear away the storm and bring out the sun?

_____

_____

_____

_____

Here is a list of problems that, in retrospect, turned into a gift:

1._____

_____

2._____

_____

3._____

_____

4._____

_____

5._____

_____

6._____

_____

7._____

_____

8._____

_____

What is bothering me?

_____

_____

_____

_____

What are the effects of this issue on me—mentally, physically, and emotionally?

_____

_____

_____

_____

What is the effect of the issue on those around me?

_____

_____

_____

_____

What does the issue cause me to do or not do?

_____

_____

_____

_____

What are the advantages of these effects, with respect to living my dream?

_____

_____

_____

_____

What are the disadvantages of these effects, with respect to living my dream?

_____

_____

_____

_____

How would life be different if the issue were gone?

_____

_____

_____

_____

Why do I need the issue?

_____

_____

_____

_____

_____

What beliefs do I have that explain how this issue might have developed?

_____

_____

_____

_____

_____

What are the payoffs for keeping the status quo regarding this issue?

_____

_____

_____

Where am I?

_____

_____

_____

Is this where I consciously choose to be?

_____

_____

_____

If not, what's my payoff?

_____

_____

_____

What action will I take to make another choice?

_____

_____

_____

If the time is not right for me to make my change, what conditions am I waiting for?

_____

_____

_____

_____

When will the time be right?

_____

_____

Is my dream greater than all my other considerations?

_____

_____

Here is a list of healthy payoffs to practice:

1. _____
2. _____
3. _____
4. _____
5. _____
6. _____
7. _____
8. _____

How many days a year will I need to take off from work activities not connected to my dream, dedicated to my well-being?

_____

What will I use my days for?

_____

_____

Will I expect to be reimbursed for these days? How will I work out a way to be paid?

_____

_____

_____

These are the ways in which I will reward myself for wellness:

1. _____
2. _____
3. _____
4. _____
5. _____
6. _____
7. _____
8. _____

How will I treat myself in a special way on my well days?

_____

_____

_____

What action will I take when body symptoms begin to send me messages that my wellness may be in jeopardy?

_____

_____

_____

How will I enroll others in my wellness?

_____

_____

What arrangements will I make with my employees and co-workers, to accommodate my wellness policy?

_____

_____

What will I do to enroll others in their own good health?

_____

_____

What was going on in my life the last three times I got sick?

1._____

_____

2._____

_____

3._____

_____

What was the payoff for the last three times I got sick?

1._____

_____

2._____

_____

3._____

_____

Did the sickness bring about the desired payoff?

1._____

2._____

3._____

Would there have been an alternative way to reach that goal?

1._____

2._____

3._____

What can I learn from this?

_____

_____

_____

What do I want?

_____

_____

_____

When do I want it?

_____

_____

_____

Am I willing to take action?

_____

_____

At what point will I definitely take action?

_____

_____

_____

What possible actions could I take?

_____

_____

_____

What specific actions will I take, by what specific times?

_____

_____

_____

How will I know when I have what I want?

_____

_____

What is my payoff for not having what I want?

_____

_____

How will I reward myself with an equal or even greater payoff for having what I want?

_____

_____

Here are three situations in which my thoughts and choice of words left me powerless and may have shut off communication:

1._____

_____

2._____

_____

3._____

_____

How could my thoughts and choice of words have been different so that these situations would have made me feel effective and in control?

1._____

_____

2._____

_____

3._____

_____

Here is a list of "Dead Words" that I use:

1._____

2._____

3._____

4._____

5._____

6._____

7._____

8._____

Here is a list of "Alive Words" that I can use as a substitution:

1._____

2._____

3._____

4._____

5._____

6._____

7._____

8._____

How do I feel when I use "Dead Words"?

_____

_____

How do I feel when I use "Alive Words"?

_____

_____

How do I feel when others use "Dead Words" with me?

_____

_____

My strengths are:

1._____

2._____

3._____

4._____

5._____

6._____

7._____

8._____

My potential abilities and strengths are:

1._____

2._____

3._____

4._____

5._____

6._____

7._____

8._____

Here is a list of positive strength statements that replace any old negative ideas and beliefs about myself:

1._____

2._____

3._____

4._____

5._____

6._____

7._____

8._____

Do I sometimes punish myself?

_____

How do I punish myself?

_____

_____

_____

For what do I punish myself?

_____

_____

How can I accomplish my purposes by loving myself more instead of punishing myself?

_____

_____

_____

In chapter 5 you enabled yourself to be the authority for your own life. When you work from the position of your strengths, you begin to live from the full array of your potential. You move out of the problem-solving mode into the creative process.

Chapter 5 Dreamwork Checklist

✓ Keep up reading and reviewing your workbook.
✓ Continue completing things and working on your dream plans.
✓ Write the story of your problem from the point of view of a third person.
✓ Find and receive the gift in every problem situation.
✓ Examine your problems or issues.
✓ Identify the payoffs related to an issue.
✓ Release your energy into constructive channels.
✓ Write parallel stories about your life in two years.
✓ Write about the payoffs of illness and what your alternatives are.
✓ Develop your own wellness policy.
✓ Keep asking, "What do I want?"
✓ Make a flow chart plan for getting what you want.
✓ Watch your words—use alive, not dead, language.
✓ Ask your partner to catch you using "Alive Words" and compliment you.
✓ Turn your weaknesses into strengths.
✓ Stop punishing yourself—appreciate and learn.
✓ Choose to change your focus from problems to solutions.
✓ Turn your negatives into positives; choose to move on and enjoy!

CHAPTER 6

....

Dare to Stretch and Expand

When you decide to be all you are, you come to the realization that stretching and expanding is a requirement and that it is also a lifelong process. There is always more to learn and more to become. Our only limit is our own willingness to grow. To fully live your dream, you need to do whatever it takes. The steps required are not always easy, but the rewards are incredible. Sounds like hard work, doesn't it? But if you are fully committed to living your dream, you will be working harder than ever before and enjoying it more.

If you are continuing to stretch and expand, you may be experiencing some growing pains. The journaling questions in this chapter will take you through the necessary steps that are a part of becoming all of who you are. You'll learn how to advance your dream by reviewing your progress so far, acknowledging yourself, enrolling in a support system, keeping yourself free from incompletes, experiencing yourself in a larger way, and taking full ownership for everything that happens in your life.

Remember as you reflect and journal that you are at a critical point in your dreamwork. You are headed toward celebration! Your new shoes are being broken in—soon they will feel so natural that you'll run and dance freely in them. But this is a point where many people give up if they have not built adequate self-reinforcing rewards and supports into their program for growth. It's especially important to the realization of your dream, then, that you are fully committed to advancing your dream. Are you ready to progress to the next level, to leave behind your reticence and excuses and do whatever it takes to stay committed?

Good! Then let's move forward!

Am I willing to stretch?

_____

Am I willing to be uncomfortable?

_____

Am I willing to be an unlimited person?

_____

Here are some notes of the actual, concrete progress I have made since I began living my dream:

_____

_____

_____

_____

_____

What changes have I made?

_____

_____

_____

_____

How is my life different now?

_____

_____

_____

_____

Here is a summary of my "Live Your Dream" process so far:

_____

_____

_____

_____

_____

What do I need for empowerment and support?

_____

_____

Who do I want to empower and support me?

_____

_____

How can I organize a support system for myself?

_____

_____

_____

_____

Here is a list of eight things, taken from a miserable stance of "I have to's":

1. I have to _____

2. I have to _____

3. I have to _____

4. I have to _____

5. I have to _____

6. I have to _____

7. I have to _____

8. I have to _____

Here is a list of the same eight things shifted from the miserable "I have to" mode to the stretch and expand mode of "I get to":

1. I get to _____

2. I get to _____

3. I get to _____

4. I get to _____

5. I get to _____

6. I get to _____

7. I get to _____

8. I get to _____

Are there any things I've let remain incomplete?

_____

_____

_____

How has this incompleteness made me feel?

_____

_____

_____

Here is a list of items from chapter 3 that I have yet to complete:

1._____

2._____

3._____

4._____

5. _____
6. _____
7. _____
8. _____

What questions do I need to ask myself about these items?

1. _____
2. _____
3. _____
4. _____
5. _____
6. _____
7. _____
8. _____

What is stopping me from completing these items?

1. _____
2. _____
3. _____
4. _____
5. _____
6. _____
7. _____
8. _____

What do I have to do to complete these items?

1. _____

_____

2. _____

_____

3. _____

_____

4. _____

_____

5. _____

_____

6. _____

_____

7. _____

_____

8. _____

_____

How will I be closer to living my dream once these items are completed?

1. _____
2. _____
3. _____
4. _____
5. _____
6. _____
7. _____
8. _____

What excuses come to mind about why these items are not completed?

1. _____
2. _____

3. _____

4. _____

5. _____

6. _____

7. _____

8. _____

What is the push that will get me through these excuses to completion?

1. _____

2. _____

3. _____

4. _____

5. _____

6. _____

7. _____

8. _____

What do I really want—excuses or results?

_____

Is the image I am putting out consistent with my dream?

_____

In what ways is the image I am putting out inconsistent with my dream?

_____

_____

_____

_____

What can I do to change the image I am putting out to align it with my dream?

_____

_____

_____

_____

_____

What is the new image I will put out when it aligns with my dream?

_____

_____

_____

_____

_____

What items can I change in my environment to make them align with my dream?

1._____
2._____
3._____
4._____
5._____
6._____
7._____
8._____

How will I change these items in my environment to make them align with my dream?

1._____

_____

2._____

3. _____

4. _____

5. _____

6. _____

7. _____

8. _____

Here are five belief statements that tell the highest truth about me, canceling out previous ideas about whatever I thought was holding me back in the category of habits:

1. _____
2. _____
3. _____
4. _____
5. _____

Here are five belief statements that tell the highest truth about me, canceling out previous ideas about whatever I thought was holding me back in the category of beliefs:

1. _____
2. _____
3. _____
4. _____
5. _____

Here are five belief statements that tell the highest truth about me, canceling out previous ideas about whatever I thought was holding me back in the category of persons:

1. _____
2. _____
3. _____
4. _____
5. _____

Here are five belief statements that tell the highest truth about me, canceling out previous ideas about whatever I thought was holding me back in the category of things:

1. _____
2. _____
3. _____
4. _____
5. _____

Here are five belief statements that tell the highest truth about me, canceling out previous ideas about whatever I thought was holding me back in the category of motivators:

1. _____
2. _____
3. _____
4. _____
5. _____

Here are five belief statements that tell the highest truth about me, canceling out previous ideas about whatever I thought was holding me back in the category of values:

1. _____
2. _____
3. _____

4._____

5._____

What words would I use to describe the major life shift I am making from the person I used to be to the person I want to become?

_____

_____

_____

An imaginary dream workshop is an ideal solution for creating This is how I envision the exterior surroundings:

_____

_____

_____

_____

_____

This is how I envision my ideal door to my imaginary dream workshop:

_____

_____

_____

What are the walls made of in my imaginary dream workshop?

_____

_____

What does the floor look like in my imaginary dream workshop?

_____

_____

Are there windows in my imaginary dream workshop? How many and where are they placed? What type of windows are they? What kind of view do they give?

_____

_____

_____

_____

_____

_____

What answer is on the feedback sheet which my workshop computer has just printed out?

_____

_____

What am I wearing that best supports my dream?

_____

_____

Who is on my video screen in the video area of my dream workshop?

_____

_____

What message do these people have for me?

_____

_____

What gift does each person bring me?

_____

_____

As my entire dream unfolds on the video screen, like a plot to a movie, I watch and see myself living my dream. What title do I choose for my dream in this "movie"?

_____

_____

In detail, what does my special place for doing the work required to create my dream look like?

_____

_____

_____

_____

_____

_____

Is there any special equipment I need?

_____

_____

What is the one idea that will allow me to perfectly create my dream?

_____

_____

What colors are in my special place, used just for relaxing?

_____

_____

What sounds emanate from this special place?

_____

_____

What do I want to smell in this special place?

_____

_____

What feelings do I want this special place to elicit?

_____

_____

What kind of furniture will I place here?

_____

_____

How will I design the walls, floor, and windows?

_____

_____

_____

What else would I like to add to enhance its beauty and comfort?

_____

_____

_____

What is my dream?

_____

_____

_____

_____

_____

How will my lifestyle or my way of being change, if I were living my dream right now?

_____

_____

_____

_____

_____

_____

What would be a real stretch for me to try?

1._____

2._____

3._____

4._____

5._____

6._____

7._____

8._____

What are the uncomfortable experiences that I want to grow beyond?

1._____

2._____

3._____

4._____

5._____

6._____

7._____

8._____

Chapter 6 enables you to take ownership for everything that happens. Once your life becomes about you being true to who you are, and telling your truth dauntlessly—the minute you take ownership—no one and nothing else has power over you. You, and not outside people, places, or things, are the sole shaper of your reality.

Chapter 6 Dreamwork Checklist

✓ Review your workbook. Summarize your progress so far.
✓ Acknowledge yourself!
✓ Create a support team.
✓ Shift from I have to... to I get to...
✓ Study and update complete items, and answer the questions about them.
✓ Stay current in all communications and responsibilities.
✓ Eliminate excuses.
✓ Complete all incomplete items.
✓ Expose any hidden agendas, and practice developing your new image, true to your real self.
✓ Take a toothbrush to your life.
✓ Create and use the chart of belief statements. Read these over morning and evening, and keep them always in your thoughts.
✓ Write your major life shift.
✓ Create a belief statements tape.
✓ Act As If.
✓ Make a fear list.
✓ Try something scary every day. Stretch your ideas of what you can do.
✓ Everything that happens, take ownership for your experience of it.

CHAPTER 7

·······················

Keeping the Dream Alive

It is important to do the work necessary to keep your dream alive. Reviewing what has happened and learning to think about things in a new way are important to assure that you keep growing to new levels instead of just repeating old patterns. This chapter shows you how to stay on track, how to let go of faulty thinking and choose new thoughts more in alignment with your dream. In essence, you'll learn how to step out beyond where you are and create a new reality.

The journaling questions in this chapter show you the way to get rid of your old programmed perceptions and see things differently. There are many issues and problems that may crop up as you model your life in the direction you want it to go. The following section deals with some of these issues and teaches you how to bring change through taking action. Through answering the following questions, you'll learn where to start to bring yourself closer to living your dream; how to ascertain what your true gifts are; what to do when your responsibilities are dragging you down; how to handle negative feelings; how to come to peace with your past; and what to do if your dream grows faint.

To keep creating tomorrows filled with happiness, achievement, accomplishment, and satisfaction, begin in this moment saying what you want and rewarding yourself for every thought and act you take to bring it about—including completing this workbook! Exercise determination and shift your energy whenever your thoughts and actions take a turn away from actively supporting your dream.

Stretch until your comfort zone *encompasses* living your dream. People who arrive at this stage report that, as their dream is more and more a part of their daily reality, abandoning it is harder than moving forward. Avoiding the call is more difficult than facing the possibility of rejection and *just doing it*. When new dreams come along, begin a dream board without delay. And be a courageous dreamer.

What makes my heart sing?

_____

_____

_____

In what ways has the definition of my dream changed since I began reading the "text" and answering the questions in the workbook?

_____

_____

_____

What is my dream statement now?

_____

_____

_____

What is the most important thing I have learned about myself from writing in this workbook?

_____

_____

What new habits lead me to realize my dream?

_____

_____

What new beliefs are making my dream a reality?

_____

_____

_____

What changes in me have resulted from my work on completing things?

_____

_____

_____

What remains for me to complete?

_____

_____

_____

What is my plan for completing each item I've listed?

_____

_____

_____

What issues, situations, and relationships remain that need to be resolved or dealt with so I can live my dream?

_____

_____

_____

Who are the people who are empowering me to live my dream today?

_____

_____

What are the other empowering forces in my life?

_____

_____

What is the biggest stretch I've made so far?

_____

_____

What additional stretches will I make?

_____

_____

What is the single most important thing I need to do to keep myself on track with realizing my dream?

_____

_____

What clues can I pick up from my mood or thought patterns to help me notice when I am or am not living my dream?

_____

_____

What are the greatest personal rewards I receive from living my dream?

_____

_____

Here is a list of eight actions I might take to move myself one step closer to living my dream:

1. _____

2. _____

3. _____

4. _____

5. _____

6. _____

7. _____

8. _____

After reading over my list, which action steps may require a plan for further action?

_____

_____

_____

_____

_____

_____

_____

Here is a cluster diagram of how one action might lead to others.

What exactly do I want?

1._____
2._____
3._____
4._____
5._____
6._____
7._____
8._____

What steps will I take to achieve what I want?

1._____
2._____
3._____
4._____
5._____
6._____
7._____
8._____

How might these steps fit together?

_____
_____
_____
_____

Can I pursue several of my dream steps simultaneously?

_____

Does it make sense to finish one step before I begin work on another?

_____

How much time and effort needs to go into each?

_____

_____

What approach will I take?

_____

_____

What do I really want?

_____

_____

What's it going to be like to be a person fulfilling my dream?

_____

_____

What will the benefits be?

_____

_____

_____

Who will be empowered by my realizing my dream?

_____

_____

_____

How will this affect me?

_____

_____

_____

Is my dream big enough to absorb all my energy, to command all my imagination, to use all my resources, and impact the world in an important way?

_____

Why is it important to realize my dream?

_____

_____

Here is my fantasy story in which wise sages give me the answers I have been searching for:

_____

_____

_____

_____

_____

_____

_____

Here is a list of some self-imposed approaches I have taken that have been rigid and where the focus has been firmly set upon resistance and struggle:

1. _____

2. _____

3. _____

4. _____

5. _____

6._____

7._____

8._____

Here is a list of alternative approaches:

1._____

2._____

3._____

4._____

5._____

6._____

7._____

8._____

What can I change so that I am focused on creative expression rather than structure?

_____

_____

_____

_____

Here is a list of situations and the way I can introduce creativity and flair into my approach to them:

1._____

_____

_____

2._____

_____

_____

3._____

4. _____

_____

5. _____

_____

6. _____

_____

7. _____

_____

8. _____

_____

What is my fear about?

_____

_____

_____

What am I afraid of?

_____

_____

What is the worst possible outcome?

_____

_____

_____

If my fear is on the surface, what lies underneath?

_____

_____

_____

Is the fear truly about the present experience, or does it gain power by evoking some related past experience?

_____

How is my fear protecting me?

_____

_____

How could I be safe while moving beyond my fear?

_____

_____

If someone else were telling me about this fear, what advice would I give?

_____

_____

_____

What can I do to get out of my fear and into my creativity?

_____

_____

Here are eight suggestions an expert might give me, based on the understanding he or she has obtained from my answers:

1. _____

2. _____

3. _____

4. _____

5. _____

6. _____

7. _____

8. _____

If I used the question, "Is it always going to be this hard?" what would I mean by the word " hard" ?

_____

_____

_____

What is really hard:

_____

_____

_____

My realistic assessment of what it's going to take to manage this difficulty successfully:

_____

_____

_____

Am I willing to do whatever is necessary?

_____

What am I angry about?

_____

_____

_____

_____

_____

What is underneath my anger?

_____

_____

_____

_____

My bottom-line truth about this anger and pain is:

_____

_____

_____

_____

Here is an accounting of all the disturbances of my day:

1._____

2._____

3._____

4._____

5._____

6._____

7._____

8._____

How will I use this?

_____

_____

What did I learn from this?

_____

_____

_____

What will I do?

_____

_____

_____

What action or thought can erase these disturbances?

1._____

2._____

3._____

4._____

5._____

6._____

7._____

8._____

Now that the disturbances of my day have been erased, I see myself as clear and free. I see:

_____

_____

_____

I am feeling dissatisfied because:

1. _____
2. _____
3. _____
4. _____
5. _____
6. _____
7. _____
8. _____

Have I ever experienced this before? When?

1. _____
2. _____
3. _____
4. _____
5. _____
6. _____
7. _____
8. _____

What do I want that I'm not getting?

1. _____
2. _____
3. _____
4. _____
5. _____
6. _____
7. _____
8. _____

Here is a list of times in my life when I've experienced what is missing now:

1. _____
2. _____
3. _____
4. _____
5. _____
6. _____
7. _____
8. _____

What patterns are there in this list?

_____

_____

_____

What action have I been taking to get what I want lately?

_____

_____

What situations must I put myself in to experience more of what I want?

1. _____
2. _____
3. _____
4. _____
5. _____
6. _____
7. _____
8. _____

Here are the thoughts and feelings I have about the way things are:

1._____

2._____

3._____

4._____

5._____

6._____

7._____

8._____

My ideal scene would be:

_____

_____

_____

_____

_____

_____

_____

What expectations and hopes do I have?

1._____

2._____

3._____

4._____

5._____

6._____

7._____

8._____

In what ways does my present reality differ from what I want?

_____

_____

_____

_____

_____

In summary, how can I assume responsibility for creating what I want?

1. _____

2. _____

3. _____

4. _____

5. _____

6. _____

7. _____

8. _____

How will I fit my new self into my existing reality?

_____

_____

_____

_____

What discomfort do I feel?

_____

_____

_____

_____

What do I feel like doing on impulse?

_____

_____

_____

What concrete plans can I make for achieving the result I desire?

_____

_____

_____

What from my past is blocking me from moving forward today?

_____

_____

_____

What would I choose to do if there were no blocks?

_____

_____

_____

The strengths the past has developed in me include:

1._____
2._____
3._____
4._____
5._____
6._____
7._____
8._____

The necessary learning my past has afforded me includes:

1. _____
2. _____
3. _____
4. _____
5. _____
6. _____
7. _____
8. _____

What would I have liked to receive as a child?

_____

_____

What feelings did I want when I was a child?

_____

_____

What experiences did I want to have when I was a child?

_____

_____

When I think about my childhood, the important experiences that come to my mind include:

1. _____

_____

2. _____

_____

3. _____

4. _____

5. _____

6. _____

7. _____

8. _____

What did I learn from these experiences?

1. _____
2. _____
3. _____
4. _____
5. _____
6. _____
7. _____
8. _____

What did I learn from the people that were involved in these memories?

1. _____
2. _____
3. _____
4. _____
5. _____
6. _____

7._____

8._____

What am I learning now from this memory?

1._____

2._____

3._____

4._____

5._____

6._____

7._____

8._____

How have these incidents from my past shaped me to be the person I am today?

1._____

2._____

3._____

4._____

5._____

6._____

7._____

8._____

Here are three incidents in which I was in conflict with someone or felt misunderstood by someone:

1._____

_____

2._____

_____

3. _____

_____

Here are the same three incidents written from that person's point of view, as closely as I can imagine it would be:

1. _____

_____

2. _____

_____

3. _____

_____

Here is a list of times when I have had strong feelings about something:

1. _____
2. _____
3. _____
4. _____
5. _____
6. _____
7. _____
8. _____

What were my exact feelings in these incidents?

1. _____
2. _____
3. _____
4. _____
5. _____
6. _____

7. _____
8. _____

What was the emotion tied to each of these incidents?

1. _____
2. _____
3. _____
4. _____
5. _____
6. _____
7. _____
8. _____

How did I feel about myself in each of these incidents?

1. _____
2. _____
3. _____
4. _____
5. _____
6. _____
7. _____
8. _____

How do I feel now about these past incidents?

1. _____
2. _____
3. _____
4. _____

5._____

6._____

7._____

8._____

If there are still some strong feelings about any of these past incidents, is there any action I can take?

1._____

2._____

3._____

4._____

5._____

6._____

7._____

8._____

What is being powerful?

_____

_____

When have I been powerful?

1._____

_____

2._____

_____

3._____

_____

4._____

_____

5. _____

_____

6. _____

_____

7. _____

_____

8. _____

_____

Which kind of power am I most familiar with, the power of the ego or the power of the spirit?

_____

What is it I seek to express powerfully?

_____

Can I trust myself to use my power wisely?

_____

Who is threatened by my power?

_____

How might I respond to their fear?

_____

What will my world be like when I am expressing myself openly and honestly?

_____

_____

Do I need to be needed?

_____

What is my motive in being nurturing?

_____

_____

_____

What do I expect to receive in return?

_____

_____

_____

_____

If the other person were to reject me, would it make any difference in my willingness to offer nurturing?

_____

How can I bring balance and joy into my relationships?

_____

_____

_____

How can I meet my needs without taking advantage of others?

_____

_____

_____

_____

Am I giving more than I really want to?

_____

_____

If I am in a draining relationship, why am I in it? What am I accepting? What do I think I need from that person?

_____

_____

_____

Here is a list of people who take advantage of me:

1._____
2._____
3._____
4._____
5._____
6._____
7._____
8._____

Here is a list of what I need from them:

1._____
2._____
3._____
4._____
5._____
6._____
7._____
8._____

Here is a list of people I take advantage of:

1._____
2._____
3._____
4._____
5._____
6._____
7._____
8._____

Here is a list of what I need from them:

1._____
2._____
3._____
4._____
5._____
6._____
7._____
8._____

If I were deceiving myself, what lies would I tell myself?

1._____
2._____
3._____
4._____
5._____
6._____
7._____
8._____

What is the truth I'd want to avoid knowing?

1. _____
2. _____
3. _____
4. _____
5. _____
6. _____
7. _____
8. _____

What is the image of myself I want to preserve?

_____
_____
_____
_____
_____

What would I have to admit?

_____
_____
_____
_____
_____
_____

Here is a character study of myself (as if written by an empathetic friend who truly understands me):

_____
_____

_____

_____

_____

_____

_____

_____

_____

_____

What do I really want?

1. _____
2. _____
3. _____
4. _____
5. _____
6. _____
7. _____
8. _____

How can I best achieve it?

1. _____
2. _____
3. _____
4. _____
5. _____
6. _____
7. _____
8. _____

Here is a picture of myself, divided down the middle into "the light side" and "the dark side." On each side are listed various traits that characterize that side:

Here are drawings of other people—people in my life I "can't stand." I have removed each characteristic from the dark side of my picture of myself and projected those characteristics onto these other people:

If I were a concerned counselor interviewing each of these other "intolerable" people, I would ask them these questions to arrive at an understanding of their reasons for adopting such undesirable characteristics:

1. _____

_____

2. _____

_____

3. _____

_____

4. _____

_____

5. _____

_____

6. _____

_____

7. _____

_____

8. _____

_____

A list of what I imagine their answers might be:

1. _____

_____

2. _____

_____

3. _____

_____

4. _____

5. _____

6. _____

7. _____

8. _____

A list of recommendations I would give them as a concerned counselor to help them be more effective and love themselves more:

1. _____

2. _____

3. _____

4. _____

5. _____

6. _____

7. _____

8. _____

In reclaiming each of my "dark side" characteristics and joining with each of the other "undesirable" persons I have interviewed, thanking them for the new understanding they have given me, I now draw a new picture:

This is what I see now:

_____

_____

_____

How can I make enough money to support myself, doing just what I love to do?

_____

_____

How much money do I need?

_____

How much money do I want to earn?

_____

What is my predominant need for self-expression?

_____

_____

How do I most love to express myself?

_____

_____

_____

What part do other people play in the picture?

_____

_____

_____

How do others benefit from my living my dream?

_____

_____

What are the benefits they would be happy to pay me for?

_____

_____

Where have I stopped short of what it takes?

_____

_____

Is there any part of my dream that is consistent with being irresponsible about paying my bills?

_____

What is my transition plan for moving toward living my dream and paying my bills—remaining responsible throughout this shift?

_____

_____

_____

Where am I on a timeline of living my dream from beginning to end?

_____

What have I accomplished so far, and what remains that I'm going to have to do?

_____

_____

_____

Here are these events plotted on a scale that pictures the timeline of my dream:

Do I want to get out of this slump?

_____

What's stopping me?

_____

_____

Here is a dialogue between two characters: the person who loves (or at least, has some attachments to) the slump I'm in, and the person who is chomping at the bit to get going:

_____

_____

_____

_____

_____

_____

_____

_____

What is the first person avoiding?

_____

_____

_____

What makes the second person give in to that argument?

_____

_____

_____

How will the debate be resolved, if both sides are to receive $1 million to achieve a resolution that satisfies the needs of both?

_____

_____

_____

Here is a slogan or a saying for a fortune cookie that summarizes my newfound wisdom:

_____

_____

Here is a list of behaviors in another person that cause problems for me:

1. _____

2. _____

3. _____

4. _____

5. _____

6. _____

7. _____

8. _____

Here is a list of specific changes I'd like that person to make:

1. _____

2. _____

3. _____

4. _____

5. _____

6. _____

7. _____

8. _____

How would my life be different if that person changed?

_____

_____

_____

How would I be affected by these changes?

_____

_____

How would I be different?

_____

_____

_____

How do I want to be?

_____

_____

_____

_____

What options will I choose in order to be the way I want to be, whether or not the other person changes?

1._____

2._____

3._____

4._____

5._____

6._____

7._____

8._____

Would I want to be in a relationship with me?

_____

What changes might I need to make in myself?

1._____

2._____

3._____

4._____

5._____

6._____

7._____

8._____

What changes would the other person like me to make?

1._____
2._____
3._____
4._____
5._____
6._____
7._____
8._____

What kind of agreement might we negotiate?

_____
_____
_____
_____

Does my current primary relationship support me in living my dream?

_____

What's working in this relationship?

1._____
2._____
3._____
4._____
5._____
6._____
7._____
8._____

What's not working in this relationship?

1. _____
2. _____
3. _____
4. _____
5. _____
6. _____
7. _____
8. _____

Is my partner aware of my needs and desires?

_____

Are my needs and desires important in our relationship?

_____

What do I need in this relationship?

1. _____
2. _____
3. _____
4. _____
5. _____
6. _____
7. _____
8. _____

What is the purpose of our relationship?

_____

_____

_____

_____

_____

Why does my partner want to be in a relationship with me?

_____

_____

_____

What holds me in this relationship?

1._____

2._____

3._____

4._____

5._____

6._____

7._____

8._____

Am I being completely honest with myself and with my partner?

_____

If not, what is it that it's time to communicate—what do I want my partner to know?

1._____

2._____

3._____

4._____

5._____

6. _____

7. _____

8. _____

If I stay in this relationship, what changes would need to occur in order for me to realize my dream?

1. _____

2. _____

3. _____

4. _____

5. _____

6. _____

7. _____

8. _____

What have I learned from this exercise so far?

_____

_____

_____

Here is a paragraph about a wonderful experience or a magnificent success I had, recreating the glowing feeling I had, and emphasizing my effective role in bringing it about:

_____

_____

_____

_____

_____

_____

_____

My dream statement is:

_____

_____

_____

_____

Is it time to update my dream statement or my dream plan?

_____

Here is a list of demonstrations that show I am living my dream:

1._____
2._____
3._____
4._____
5._____
6._____
7._____
8._____

I know I have the desire to live my dream because:

1._____
2._____
3._____
4._____
5._____
6._____
7._____
8._____

One measurable result I will produce today that is part of bringing my dream into reality is:

_____

_____

One measurable result I will produce tomorrow is:

_____

_____

One measurable result for the next day is:

_____

_____

One measurable result for the next day is:

_____

_____

One measurable result for the next day is:

_____

_____

One measurable result for the next day is:

_____

_____

One measurable result for the next day is:

_____

_____

What have I done so far this week to accomplish my planned results?

_____

_____

_____

What are the signs that I am experiencing my dream?

1. _____
2. _____
3. _____
4. _____
5. _____
6. _____
7. _____
8. _____

What accomplishments have I achieved in the past six months?

1. _____
2. _____
3. _____
4. _____
5. _____
6. _____
7. _____
8. _____

Which assignments did I avoid?

1. _____
2. _____

3._____

4._____

5._____

6._____

7._____

8._____

What changes am I avoiding making?

1._____

2._____

3._____

4._____

5._____

6._____

7._____

8._____

What's the big step I haven't taken yet?

_____

_____

What have I done in the past to revitalize myself?

1._____

2._____

3._____

4._____

5._____

6._____

7._____

8._____

As a final exercise, get some blank paper and retire to a quiet place. Take thirty minutes to an hour to write the story that pictures you living the dream you have claimed. Include a descriptive setting that portrays you, your feelings, your environment, and other involved characters. Incorporate your goals, values, and motivators into your plot, and write a story climax that shows how all the dream work you've done has paid off in wonderful ways.

Congratulations! You have successfully completed the *Live Your Dream Workbook*. But, now that you have "finished" the workbook, it is time to go right back and start again! Experience shows that the person who grows is the one who starts the process all over again as soon as he or she has reached the goal of one dream.

Chapter 7 Dreamwork Checklist

✓ This is your life!
✓ See it!
✓ Create it!
✓ Claim it!
✓ Celebrate it!

Now that you have benefited from Joyce Chapman's workbook, it's time to share the benefits with your friends, family, and acquaintances.

Contact Newcastle Publishing at (800) 932-4809 to order additional copies of the book. Quantity discounts are available to groups, organizations, and companies for any Newcastle title. All major credit cards accepted.

For more information on Joyce's workshops, books, consulting services, speaking engagements, and facilitating journaling groups, write to:

Joyce Chapman, M.A.
826 Orange Avenue, #111
Coronado, CA 92118